*Freemasonry,
Mithraism
and the
Ancient Mysteries*

By H. L. Haywood
C. W. Leadbeater
J. S. M. Ward
Manly P. Hall

Copyright © 2020 Lamp of Trismegistus. All rights reserved. No part of this publication may be reproduced or transmitted in any form or by any means, electronic or mechanical, including photocopying, recording, or by any information storage and retrieval system, without permission in writing from Lamp of Trismegistus. Reviewers may quote brief passages.

ISBN: 978-1-63118-407-9

*Foundations of Freemasonry
Series*

Other Books in this Series and Related Titles

Masonic and Rosicrucian History by M P Hall & H Voorhis (978-1-63118-486-4)

The Kabbalah of Masonry & Related Writings by E Levi &c (978-1-63118-453-6)

Some Deeper Aspects of Masonic Symbolism by A E Waite (978-1-63118-461-1)

Masonic Symbolism of King Solomon's Temple by A Mackey &c (978-1-63118-442-0)

The Old Past Master by Carl H Claudy (978-1-63118-464-2)

The Mysteries of Freemasonry & the Druids by various (978-1-63118-444-4)

Rosicrucians and Speculative Masonry in the Seventeenth Century (978-1-63118-489-5)

The Two Great Pillars of Boaz and Jachin by A Mackey &c (978-1-63118-433-8)

The Regius Poem or Halliwell Manuscript by King Solomon (978-1-63118-447-5)

The Lost Keys of Freemasonry or The Secret of Hiram Abiff (978-1-63118-427-7)

Masonic Symbolism of the Apron & the Altar by various (978-1-63118-428-4)

Symbolism and Discourses on the Entered Apprentice, Fellowcraft and Master Mason Blue Lodge Degrees by various (978-1-63118-413-0)

The Legend of the Holy Grail and its Connection with Templars and Freemasons by A E Waite (978-1-63118-462-8)

Freemasonry in the Medieval or Middle Ages by various (978-1-63118-450-5)

American Indian Freemasonry by A C Parker (978-1-63118-460-4)

Ancient Mysteries and Secret Societies by M P Hall (978-1-63118-410-9)

The Ceremony of Initiation: Analysis & Commentary (978-1-63118-473-4)

Masonic Life of George Washington by Albert G Mackey (978-1-63118-457-4)

The Janeites, The Man Who Would Be King and Other Stories of Freemasonry by Rudyard Kipling (978-1-63118-480-2)

Audio Versions are also available on Audible, Amazon and Apple

Table of Contents

Introduction...7

Mithraism: Freemasonry and the Ancient Mysteries
by H. L. Haywood

Introduction...9
How Mithra Came to be a First-Class God...10
How Mithra Found His Way to Rome...13
The Mithraic Theory of Things...17
In What Way Mithraism Was Like Freemasonry...20

The Mithraic Mysteries
by C. W. Leadbeater

Zarathustra and Mithraism...23
Mithraism Among the Romans...24
The Mithraic Rites...27
The Roman Collegia...30
The Work of King Numa...32
The Colleges and the Legions...35
The Introduction of the Jewish Form...37
The Transition to the Operatives...38

The System of Mithra
by J. S. M. Ward...41

The Rites of Mithras
by Manly P. Hall...51

INTRODUCTION

From the beginning of Modern Freemasonry's birthdate of 1717, the intelligentsia of humanity have found refuge for safe reflection within the walls of the fraternity. Masonic writers have produced a nearly incalculable amount of written musings on a multitude of esoteric and philosophical subjects, as they relate to the ancient mysteries that Freemasonry currently storehouses. Sadly, most of it appears to have sat largely unread, as American Freemasonry in particular, continues to transform itself into something that bears little resemblance to what it was originally designed to be. The true essence of Freemasonry is not that of blind patriotism or a single-minded national religion but one of Universal Brotherhood and altruism, designed for the betterment not just of its members but of society as a whole. In particular, for those who are not members of the fraternity, as Freemasonry has always acted as a beacon, to help guide humanity through darker times, with the hopes that one day we will collectively reach a truly enlightened age.

It's not uncommon for new members joining the fraternity to find little education within the walls of many modern lodges, in spite of so much written material available to the membership. Many older members are not simply uneducated with regards to real Masonic history and symbology, not to mention the vast arena of related subjects, but they are disinterested in all of it, as well.

Lamp of Trismegistus is doing its part to help preserve humanity's Masonic history by making some of these classics available to those students who are seeking to unearth the knowledge of these ancient colossi. As such, Lamp of Trismegistus offers its readers highlights of Masonic study, culled from a variety of authors and viewpoints, with the hope bringing education back into the fraternity. So, be sure to check out other titles in our *Foundations of Freemasonry Series* as well as our *Theosophical Classics, Occult Fiction, Paranormal Research Series, Esoteric Classics, Supernatural Fiction, Studies in Buddhism* and our *Christian Apocrypha Series* as well as numerous other subjects; and, don't be afraid to let a little altruism into your own heart or even into your Lodge. You can also download the audio versions of many of these titles from Audible, Amazon or Apple, for learning on the go.

MITHRAISM: FREEMASONRY AND THE ANCIENT MYSTERIES

by H. L. Haywood

INTRODUCTION

The theory that modern Freemasonry is m some sense a direct descendant from the ancient Mysteries has held a peculiar attraction for Masonic writers this long time, and the end is not yet, for the world is rife with men who argue about the matter up and down endless pages of print. It is a most difficult subject to write about, so that the more one learns about it the less he is inclined to ventilate any opinions of his own. The subject covers so much ground and in such tangled jungles that almost any grand generalization is pretty sure to be either wrong or useless. Even Gould, who is usually one of the soundest and carefullest of generalizers, gets pretty badly mixed up on the subject.

For present purposes it has seemed to me wise to attention to one only of the Mysteries, letting it stand as a type of the rest, and I have chosen for that purpose MITHRAISM, one of the greatest and one of most interesting, as well as one possessing as many parallelisms with Freemasonry as any of the others

I
HOW MITHRA CAME TO BE A FIRST-CLASS GOD

Way back in the beginning of things, so we may learn from the Avesta, Mithra was the young god of the sky lights that appeared just before sunrise and lingered after the sun had set. To him was attributed patronship of the virtues of truth, life-giving, and youthful strength and joy. Such qualities attracted many worshippers in whose eyes Mithra grew from more to more until finally he became a great god in his own right and almost equal to the sun god himself. "Youth will be served," even a youthful god; and Zoroastrianism, which began by giving Mithra a very subordinate place, came at last to exalt him to the right hand of the awful Ormuzd, who had rolled up within himself all the attributes of all gods whatsoever.

When the Persians conquered the Babylonians, who worshipped the stars in a most thoroughgoing manner, Mithra got himself placed at the very center of star worshipping cults, and won such strength for himself that when the Persian Empire went to pieces and everything fell into the melting pot with it, Mithra was able to hold his own identity, and emerged from the struggle at the head of a religion of his own. He was a young god full of vigour and overflowing with spirits, capable of teaching his followers the arts of victory, and such things appealed mightily to the bellicose Iranian tribesmen who never ceased to worship him in one form or another until they became so soundly converted to Mohammedanism centuries afterwards. Even then they did not abandon him altogether but after the inevitable manner of converts rebuilt him into Allah and into Mohammed, so that even today one will find pieces of Mithra scattered about here and there in what the Mohammedans call their theology.

After the collapse of the Persian Empire, Phrygia, where so many religions were manufactured at one time or another, took Mithra up and built a cult about him. They gave him his Phrygian cap which one always sees on his statues, and they incorporated in his rites the use of the dreadful "taurobolium," which was a baptism in the blood of a healthy young bull. In the course of time this gory ceremony became the very center and climax of the Mithraic ritual, and made a profound impression on the hordes of poor slaves and ignorant men who flocked into the mithrea, as the Mithraic houses of worship were called.

Mithra was never able to make his way into Greece (the same thing could be said of Egypt, where the competition among religions was very severe) but it happened that he borrowed something from Greek art. Some unknown Greek sculptor, one of the shining geniuses of his nation, made a statue of Mithra that served ever afterwards as the orthodox likeness of the god, who was depicted as a youth of overflowing vitality, his mantle thrown back, a Phrygian cap on his head, and slaying a bull. For hundreds of years this statue was to all devout Mithraists what the crucifix now is to Roman Catholics. This likeness did much to open Mithra's path toward the west, for until this his images had been hideous in the distorted and repellant manner so characteristic of Oriental religious sculpture. The Oriental people, among whom Mithra was born, were always capable of gloomy grandeur and of religious terror, but of beauty they had scarcely a touch; it remained for the Greeks to recommend Mithra to men of good taste.

After the Macedonian conquests, so it is believed, the cult of Mithra became crystallized; it got its orthodox theology, its church system, its philosophy, its dramas and rites, its picture of the universe and of the grand cataclysmic end of all things in a terrific day of judgment. Many things had been built into it. There were exciting ceremonies for the multitudes; much mysticism for the devout; a great machinery of salvation for the timid; a program of militant activity for men of valour; and a lofty ethic for the superior classes. Mithraism had a history, traditions, sacred books, and a vast momentum from the worship of millions and millions among remote and scattered tribes. Thus accoutered and equipped, the young god and his religion were prepared to enter the more complex and sophisticated world known as the Roman Empire.

II
HOW MITHRA FOUND HIS WAY TO ROME

When Mithridates Eupator - he who hated the Romans with a virulency like that of Hannibal, and who waged war on them three or four times - was utterly destroyed in 66 B.C. and his kingdom of Pontus was given over to the dogs, the scattered fragments of his armies took refuge among the outlaws and pirates of Cilicia and carried with them everywhere the rites and doctrines of Mithraism. Afterwards the soldiers of the Republic of Tarsus, which these outlaws organized, went pillaging and fighting all round the Mediterranean, and carried the cult with them everywhere. It was in this unpromising manner that Mithra made his entrance into the Roman world. The most ancient of all inscriptions is one made by a freedman of the Flavians at about this time.

In the course of time Mithra won to his service a very different and much more efficient army of missionaries. Syrian merchants went back and forth across the Roman world like shuttles in a loom, and carried the new cult with them wherever they went. Slaves and freedmen became addicts and loyal supporters. Government officials, especially those belonging to the lowlier ranks, set up altars at every opportunity. But the greatest of all the propagandists were the soldiers of the various Roman armies. Mithra, who was believed to love the sight of glittering swords and flying banners, appealed irresistibly to soldiers, and they in turn were as loyal to him as to any commander on the field. The time came when almost every Roman camp possessed its mithreum.

Mithra began down next to the ground but the time came when he gathered behind him the great ones of the earth. Antoninus Pius, father-in-law of Marcus Aurelius, erected a Mithraic temple at Ostia, seaport of the city of Rome. With the exception of Marcus Aurelius and possibly one or two others all the pagan emperors after Antoninus were devotees of the god, especially Julian, who was more or less addle-pated and willing to take up with anything to stave off the growing power of Christianity. The early Church Fathers nicknamed Julian "The Apostate"; the slur was not altogether just because the young man had never been a Christian under his skin.

Why did all these great fellows, along with the philosophers and literary men who obediently followed suit, take up the worship of a foreign god, imported from amidst the much hated Syrians, when there were so many other gods of home manufacture so close at hand? Why did they take to a religion that had been made fashionable by slaves and cutthroats? The answer is easy to discover. Mithra was peculiarly fond of rulers and of the mighty of the earth. His priests declared that the god himself stood at the right hand of emperors both on and off the throne. It was these priests who invented the good old doctrine of the divine right of kings. The more Mithra was worshipped by the masses, the more complete was the imperial control of those masses, therefore it was good business policy for the emperors to give Mithra all the assistance they could. There came a time when every Emperor was pictured by the artists with a halo about his head; that halo had origin ally belonged to Mithra. It represented the outstanding splendour of the young and vigorous sun. After the Roman emperors passed away the popes and bishops of the Roman Catholic Church took up the custom; they are still in the habit of showing their saints be-haloed.

Mithraism spread up and down the world with amazing rapidity. All along the coast of northern Africa and even in the recesses of the Sahara; through the Pillars of Hercules to England and up into Scotland; across the channel into Germany and the north countries; and down into the great lands along the Danube, he everywhere made his way. London was at one time a great center of his worship. The greatest number of mithrea were built in Germany. Ernest Renan once said that if ever Christianity had become s mitten by a fatal malady Mithraism might very easily: have become the established and official religion of the whole Western World. Men might now be saying prayers to Mithra, and have their children baptised in bull's blood.

There is not here space to describe in what manner the cult became modified, by its successful spread across the Roman Empire. It was modified, of course, and in many ways profoundly, and it in turn modified everything with which it came into contact.

Here is a brief epitome of the evolution of this Mystery. It began at a remote time among primitive Iranian tribesmen. It picked up a body of doctrine from the Babylonian star worshippers, who created that strange thing known as astrology. It became a mystery, equipped with powerful rites, in the Asia Minor countries. It received a decent outward appearance at the hand of Greek artists and philosophers; and it finally became a world religion among the Romans. Mithraism reached its apogee in the second century; it went the way of all flesh in the fourth century; and flickered out entirely in the fifth century, except that bits of its wreckage were salvaged and used by a few new cults, such as those of the various forms of Manichaeism.

III
THE MITHRAIC THEORY OF THINGS

After overthrowing its hated rival, the early Christian Church so completely destroyed everything having to do with Mithraism that there have remained behind but few fragments to bear witness to a once victorious religion. What little is accurately known will be found all duly set down and correctly interpreted in the works of the learned Dr. Franz Cumont, whose books on the subject so aroused the ire of the present Roman Catholic Hierarchy that they placed them on the Index, and warned the faithful away from his chapters of history. Today, as in Mithra's time, superstitions and empty doctrines have a sorry time when confronted with known facts.

The pious Mithraist believed that back of the stupendous scheme of things was a great and unknowable deity, Ormuzd by name, and that Mithra was his son. A soul destined for its prison house of flesh left the presence of Ormuzd, descended by the gates of Cancer, passed through the spheres of the seven planets and in each of these picked up some function or faculty for use on the earth. After its term here the soul was prepared by sacraments and discipline for its re-ascent after death. Upon its return journey it underwent a great ordeal of judgment before Mithra. Leaving something behind it in each of the planetary spheres it finally passed back through the gates of Capricorn to ecstatic union with the great Source of all. Also there was an eternal hell, and those who had proved unfaithful to Mithra were sent there. Countless demons, devils and other invisible monsters raged about everywhere over the earth tempting souls, and presided over the tortures in the pit. Through it all the planets continued to exercise good or evil influence over the human being, according as his fates might chance to fall out on high, a thing imbedded in the cult from its old Babylonian days.

The life of a Mithraist was understood as a long battle in which, with Mithra's help, he did war against the principles and powers of evil. In the beginning of his life of faith he was purified by baptism, and through all his days received strength through sacraments and sacred meals. Sunday was set aside as a holy day, and the twenty-fifth of December began a season of jubilant celebration. Mithraic priests were organized in orders, and were deemed to have supernatural power to some extent or other.

MITHRAS SLAYING THE BULL

It was believed that Mithra had once come to earth in order to organize the faithful into the army of Ormuzd. He did battle with the Spirit of all Evil in a cave, the Evil taking the form of a bull. Mithra overcame his adversary and then returned to his place on high as the leader of the forces of righteousness, and the judge of all the dead. All Mithraic ceremonies centered about the bull slaying episode.

The ancient Church Fathers saw so many points of resemblance between this cult and Christianity that many of them accepted the theory that Mithraism was a counterfeit religion devised by Satan to lead souls astray. Time has proved them to be wrong in this because at bottom Mithraism was as different from Christianity as night from day.

IV
IN WHAT WAY MITHRAISM WAS LIKE FREEMASONRY

Masonic writers have often professed to see many points of resemblance between Mithraism and Freemasonry. Albert Pike once declared that Freemasonry is the modern heir of the Ancient Mysteries. It is a dictum with which I have never been able to agree. There are similarities between our Fraternity and the old Mystery Cults, but most of them are of a superficial character, and have to do with externals of rite or, organization, and not with inward content. When Sir Samuel Dill described Mithraism as "a sacred Freemasonry" he used that name in a very loose sense. Nevertheless, the resemblances are often startling. Men only were admitted to membership in the cult. "Among the hundreds of inscriptions that have come down to us, not one mentions either a priestess, a woman initiate, or even a donatress." In this the mithrea differed from the collegia, which latter, though they almost never admitted women as members, never hesitated to accept help or money from them. Membership in Mithraism was as democratic as it is with us, perhaps more so; slaves were freely admitted and often held positions of trust, as also did the freedmen of whom there were such multitudes in the latter centuries of the empire.

Membership was usually divided into seven grades, each of which had its own appropriate symbolical ceremonies. Initiation was the crowning experience of every worshipper. He was attired symbolically, took vows, passed through many baptisms, and in the higher grades ate sacred meals with his fellows. The great event of the initiate's experiences was the taurobolium, already described. It was deemed very efficacious, and was supposed to unite the worshipper with Mithra himself. A dramatic representation of a dying and a rising again was at the head of all these ceremonies. A tablet showing in bas relief Mithra's killing of the bull stood at the end of every mithreum.

This, mithreum, as the meeting place, or lodge, was called, was usually cavern shaped, to represent the cave in which the god had his struggle. There were benches or shelves along the side, and on these side lines the members sat. Each mithreum had its own officers, its president, trustees, standing committees, treasurer, and so forth, and there were higher degrees granting special privileges to the few. Charity and Relief were universally practised and one Mithraist hailed another as "brother." The Mithraic "lodge" was kept small, and new lodges were developed as a result of "swarming off" when membership grew too large.

Manichaeism, as I have already said, sprang fr the ashes of Mithraism, and St. Augustine, who did so much to give shape to the Roman Catholic church and theology was for many years an ardent Manichee, an through him many traces of the old Persian creed found their way into Christianity. Out of Manichaeism, or out of what was finally left of it, came Paulicianism, and out of Paulicianism came many strong medieval cults - the Patari, the Waldenses, the Hugenots, and countless other such developments. Through these various channels echoes of the old Mithraism persisted over Europe, and it may very well be, as has often been alleged, that there are faint traces of the ancient cult to be found here and there in our own ceremonies or symbolisms. Such theories are necessarily vague and hard to prove, and anyway the thing is not of sufficient importance to argue about. If we have three or four symbols that originated in the worship of Mithra, so much the better for Mithra!

After all is said and done the Ancient Mysteries were among the finest things developed in the Roman world. They stood for equality in a savagely aristocratic and class-riddled society; they offered centers of refuge to the poor and the despised among a people little given to charity and who didn't believe a man should love his neighbour; and in a large historical way they left behind them methods of human organization, ideals and principles and hopes which yet remain in the world for our use and profit. It a man wishes to do so, he may say that what Freemasonry is among us, the Ancient Mysteries were to the people of the Roman world, but it would be a difficult thing for any man to establish the fact that Freemasonry has directly descended from those great cults.

THE MITHRAIC MYSTERIES

By C. W. Leadbeater

ZARATHUSTRA AND MITHRAISM

The Mysteries of Mithra were in many ways similar to those of Greece, but they always had certain characteristics which were especially their own, and the line of succession which they transmitted was distinct from that of the three degrees of Blue Masonry; some of the more important features of its ritual seem to have passed over into the 18°. There was a strong military flavour about them, and they demanded from their devotees a purity of life which was almost ascetic.

Just as the Mysteries of Egypt and Greece arose respectively from the incarnations of the World Teacher as Thoth and Orpheus, so did the Mithraic scheme arise from His incarnation as the first Zarathustra about 29,700 B.C. in Persia. It taught of Mithra, Captain of the hosts of the God of Light and Saviour of mankind.

MITHRAISM AMONG THE ROMANS

It is said that Mithraism was first transmitted to the Roman world during the first century B.C. by the Cilician pirates captured by Pompey; but, as we have already seen, it was before that time in the possession of the Essene communities in Palestine. For nearly two centuries it attained no great importance in Rome, and it was not until the end of the first century A.D. that it began to attract serious attention. Towards the close of the second century, the cult had spread rapidly through the army, the mercantile class and the slaves, all of which classes were largely composed of Asiatics. It throve especially at the military posts, and in the track of trade, where its monuments have been discovered in greatest abundance. Some twenty of the Mithraic temples still remain, and they show certain points of resemblance to our Masonic Lodges. The temple was rectangular, with a raised platform at the east end, often apsidal in form; continuous benches ran along its walls on the longer sides for the accommodation of the Brn., and the ceiling was made to symbolize the firmament.

Jerome (Epist. cvii) tells us that the system consisted of seven degrees: Corax, the Raven, so-called not only because the raven was the servant of the sun in Mithraic mythology, but because the raven can only imitate speech and not originate ideas for himself;* (*Cf. the Akoustikoi of the Pytagoreans, and the fact that the due-gard of the 1° shows that the E.A. must confine himself to what is taught in the V.S.L.) Cryphius, the Occult, a degree in the taking of which the mystic was perhaps hidden from others in the sanctuary by a veil, the removal of which was a solemn ceremonial; Miles, the Soldier, signifying the holy warfare against evil in the service of the God; Leo, the Lion, symbolic of the element of fire, which played so great a part in the Persian faith; Perses, the Persian, clad in Asiatic costume, a reminiscence of the ancient origin of the religion; Heliodromus, the Courier of the Sun, with whom Mithra was identified; and Pater, the Father, a degree bringing the mystic among those who had the general direction of the cult for the rest of their lives.

It is not easy to trace exact correspondences between these seven stages and our own degrees, because of the difference between the systems. The Corax is fairly parallel with the E.A., and the Cryphius and Miles with the F.C., the latter being distinguished from the former by additional knowledge which may not inaptly be compared with that of the Mark degree. These three classes together were regarded to some extent as servitors; the next stage, Leo, was the first whose members were called "participants" and admitted to the Mithraic sacrament. We may consider the three stages of Leo, Perses and Heliodromus as divisions of the M.M. degree; the first gave access to the full fellowship of the Mithraic brotherhood, the second passed him who received it through a most impressive ceremony in the course of which he was symbolically slain and raised to life in honour of Mithra, and the third put him in possession of additional knowledge equivalent to that which is supposed to be given to us in the Holy Royal Arch; for only when he had that knowledge of the name and qualities of the deity was he fitted to go forth as a messenger of the Sun to bear his strength and life through the world. The Pater corresponded to our I.M., who alone can confer the various degrees and pass on the succession to posterity.

THE MITHRAIC RITES

The Mithraic cult was essentially a religion of soldiers, a veritable brotherhood of arms. Women were never admitted to their rites of initiation, although it seems probable that in earlier times there were separate degrees for them. The power flowing through the rites gave especially courage and purity, and the demands upon the candidates in both these respects were exceedingly high. There was an intensity of brotherly feeling between the initiates of Mithra which is rarely realized in our Lodges today; they were pledged to fight for the right, and they stood shoulder to shoulder against all foes.

The Mithraic sacrament consisted of bread and wine and salt, and was consecrated at a solemn ceremony in the Mysteries, being linked to that aspect of the Deity which was represented by Mithra, and intensely charged with force along the characteristic lines of purity, courage and brotherhood, helping to bind the brethren together into a body corporate as soldiers of Light and Truth. This same Eucharist has been transmitted to us today through the Culdee line of tradition, in the ceremonial of the Rose-Croix of Heredom; but the forces flowing through it have been modified to some extent, so that instead of a Brotherhood of Arms we have now a Brotherhood of Love. The power of love takes the place of the military influence of courage, although the method of consecration in the higher worlds is the same. This is due to a blending with the Egyptian line of tradition.

The analogies between Mithraism and Christianity are very close; they are well summarized thus in the Encyclopedia Britannica:

The fraternal and democratic spirit of the first communities, and their humble origin; the identification of the object of adoration with light and the Sun; the legends of the shepherds with their gifts and adoration, the flood, and the ark; the representation in art of the fiery chariot, the drawing of water from the rock; the use of bell and candle, holy water and the communion; the sanctification of Sunday and of the 25th of December; the insistence on moral conduct, the emphasis placed upon abstinence and self-control; the doctrine of heaven and hell, of primitive revelation, of the mediation of the Logos emanating from the divine, the atoning sacrifice, the constant warfare between good and evil and the final triumph of the former, the immortality of the soul, the last judgment, the resurrection of the flesh and the fiery destruction of the universe - these are some of the resemblances ... At their root lay a common Eastern origin rather than any borrowing?*
(*Ency. Brit. (11th Edn.), Art. Mithras.)

The Great Powers behind evolution appear at one time to have thought seriously of making Mithraism the religion of the fifth sub-race instead of the maimed Christianity which had rejected its own gnosis and put aside its Mysteries. But the ideal of Mithraic purity was so high that it would probably have been impossible for men to follow it during the Dark Ages; and another very serious objection to the system was that it absolutely excluded women. Mithraism was allowed therefore to sink into the background and finally to pass out of sight of the outer world. Nevertheless the ancient succession is still guarded and the rites are preserved in the custody of the H.O.A.T.F.; so Mithraism may yet have its part to play in the religious life of the future.

In addition to the Mysteries of Mithra, there was an Atlantean tradition of the Mysteries - that to which we have already referred as the Chaldaean line of succession. In the days of its splendour the Chaldaean rituals put the initiate into relation with the great Star-Angels who were adored in that mighty faith; and a relic of this tradition is still found in the hidden side of certain of the degrees of the rites of Memphis and of Mizraim. The Chaldaean method of seating the Principal Officers of a Lodge is still preserved in Continental Masonry, and has passed also into certain of the higher degrees.

THE ROMAN COLLEGIA

We may now return to the main line of Masonic descent, that of the three Craft degrees. We have already seen how the Jewish Mysteries handed down the essentials of our Masonic rites; it remains for us to trace their transmission to our modern Lodges. The next link in the chain is the Roman Collegia, in which the transition from speculative to operative Masonry took place.

We have seen that the science of architecture was always closely connected with the Mysteries, and that our Masonic Craft ritual when properly worked is designed to build a superphysical temple of the Ionic order of architecture, which was chosen because it is the vehicle of the special type of force which flows through Craft Masonry.* (*See The Hidden Life in Freemasonry, p. 120.)

Other forms are built by the higher degrees, belonging to different kinds of architecture, according to the influences which are to be radiated through them; so we see that we are in the presence of a science of spiritual building, of which material architecture is but the reflection in the dense matter of the physical plane. Each order of architecture expresses an idea and is the channel of certain types of influence associated with that idea, attracting the attention of certain kinds of Angels who work along the lines of that idea in the invisible worlds. Each sub-race has its own characteristic type of architecture as well as its own type of music, and these are often utilized by the

Great Ones behind in order to impress upon the people certain characteristics which are necessary for their evolution.

The principles of this inner science of building were taught in the ancient Mysteries, and the temples of the different faiths were planned by the priests with full knowledge of the hidden side of what they were doing; it was for this reason that builders were always associated with temples and temple-worship, and the secrets of building were carefully guarded as part of the teaching of the Mysteries. Thus the confusion between speculative and operative, which was purposely effected at the breaking-up of the Roman Empire, presented no difficulties to the Powers behind, since those two aspects had always worked in close association, and it was merely a question of emphasizing the one, and of temporarily withdrawing the other into yet further silence and secrecy. No essential change was required.

THE WORK OF KING NUMA

Plutarch tells us that the Roman Collegia were originally founded by Numa, the second king of Rome, who lived during the seventh century B.C.* (*Plutarch's Life of Numa, A. H. Clough, Vol. i, p. 152.) Numa is a half-legendary figure to our modern historians; but he was a very real personage, and the true founder of the Roman Mysteries as well as of the trade guilds. Plutarch says of his character:

He was endued with a soul rarely tempered by nature and disposed to virtue, which he had yet more subdued by discipline, a severe life, and the study of philosophy ... He banished all luxury and softness from his own home, and, while citizens alike and strangers found in him an incorruptible judge and counsellor, in private he devoted himself not to amusement or lucre, but to the worship of the immortal Gods, and the rational contemplation of their divine power and nature.* (*Ibid., pp. 130, 131.)

Numa was "deeply versed, so far as anyone could be in that age, in all law, divine and human,* (*Livy., Bk. I, xviii (Loeb Ed.)) says Livy; while Dio Cassius tells us that he shaped the political and peaceable institutions of Rome, as Romulus had determined its military career.* (*Dio's Roman History, Loeb. Ed., p. 29.) In addition to all his external ability, he was far advanced on the Path of Holiness, and was a high Initiate of the White Lodge. His especial work was laying down, at the very beginning of the Roman State, the inner foundation of

Rome's future greatness; he moulded both her outer religion and her inner Mysteries, which in later days were to be the channel of that spiritual force which would make Rome mighty among the nations, one of the greatest empires that the world has ever known.

Numa sent messengers to Egypt, to Greece, to Chaldaea, to Palestine and other lands, to study all existing systems of the Mysteries, so that he might adopt in Rome those most suited to the development of his people. His high occult rank opened all doors; and like Pythagoras, an even greater Initiate, who came later, he was enabled to synthesize many lines of tradition into one comprehensive whole. The system which appears to have been adopted in Rome was that of the Mysteries of Dionysus or Bacchus, which, as we have already seen, closely corresponded to the Egyptian system; and here we have the first of the links with the Dionysian Artificers of whom Masonic tradition so persistently speaks.

Numa introduced the Egyptian line of succession, and thus the hierophants of his Mysteries were I.M.s. after the manner of the priests of Egypt and the Masons of today. This succession appears to have been handed down in secret among the Colleges of Architects until the time when Christianity began to dominate the Roman world at the beginning of the third century A.D. The fortunes of the Colleges or guilds which were thus formed were very varied; gradually they rose to great political power, were abolished by the senate about 80 B.C., and restored again twenty years later. The Emperors issued edicts against them from time to time, but those which could prove their antiquity or religious character were permitted to remain in existence. They were finally abolished in A.D. 378.

THE COLLEGES AND THE LEGIONS

Of these Colleges of Architects one was attached to every Roman Legion, building for it fortifications in time of war and in time of peace temples and houses. It was thus that the Roman Mysteries were brought to Northern Europe. Wherever the Romans settled, the Collegia worked their rites, and in process of time native soldiers were initiated into their ranks, until the system became deeply-rooted in each Roman colony. Closely connected with these rites were those of Mithra which, as we have seen, were also spread by the Roman armies, although the two systems were always kept separate and distinct.

The organization of the Colleges, as extant records show, corresponded in many ways with that of our modern Lodges. "Tres faciunt Collegium" – "Three make a College" was one of their principles; and the rule was so indispensable that it became a maxim of civil law. The College was ruled by a Magister or Master, and two Decuriones or Wardens; and among other officers were a treasurer, sub-treasurer, secretary and archivist.* (*R. F. Gould, History of Freemasonry, Vol. I, p. 42.) There was also a Sacerdos or Chaplain, who was in charge of the religious side of the work. The members of the College consisted of three grades corresponding closely to Apprentices, Fellows and Masters; and records point to the fact that they possessed semi-religious rites which were kept rigidly secret, and also that they attached symbolic interpretations to their tools, such as the square and compasses, the plumb-rule and level. They took pagan gods as their patrons in much the same way as the guilds which succeeded them adopted Christian patron saints. The Four Crowned Martyrs, the patron saints of Masonry, were Christian members of a College who were tortured to death by the Emperor Diocletian for refusing to make a statue of Aesculapius.* (*J. S. M. Ward: Freemasonry and the Ancient Gods, pp. 144, 145.) They were later confused with the tradition of the Four Brothers of Horus.

Bro. J. S. M. Ward describes a building of the Collegia unearthed at Pompeii in 1878, which had been buried in A.D. 79, during the great eruption of Mount Vesuvius. It contains striking Masonic correspondences. There are two columns, and on the walls are interlaced triangles. Upon a pedestal in the centre was found an inlaid marble slab with a skull, level and plumb-rule and other Masonic designs in mosaic work. A fresco in another building close by shows a figure in the act of making the F.C.H.S.* (*J. S. M. Ward: Freemasonry and the Ancient Gods, pp. 115, 116.) The Roman Colleges of Architects were brought to Britain by the Roman army. One legion under Julius Caesar established a colony at Eboracum or York, later to be so prominent in Masonic legend and tradition; and another centre was at Verulam, afterwards known as S. Albans.

THE INTRODUCTION OF THE JEWISH FORM

The introduction of the Jewish form of the Masonic ceremonies was intentionally arranged by the Powers who stand behind Freemasonry about the time when Christianity was gaining ascendancy in the Roman Empire. It would have been almost impossible to continue the Mysteries of Bacchus or those of Mithra in their original form, while there was so much opposition between the Christian faith and the old Pagan religion. No such opposition was in Roman days felt towards the Jews, among whom the Christian faith arose and had its early nurture; and the Jewish form of the Mysteries was therefore adopted by the White Lodge as the best means of transmitting the ancient rites through the Dark Ages, when the Church rigorously persecuted all who were not in agreement with her doctrines. The chief agent in the work of transition was He who was then known as S. Alban, but whom today we revere as the Master the Comte de S. Germain, the Head of all true Freemasons throughout the world. I have given some account of Him and His Roman incarnation in The Hidden Life in Freemasonry.* (*Op. cit., pp. 12-16)

THE TRANSITION TO THE OPERATIVES

The Mysteries of Bacchus quite naturally and gradually gave place to the Jewish form of the same tradition as Christianity grew more and more powerful; for this was not incompatible with the Christian faith as the Greek and Egyptian traditions would have been; and the speculative secrets were more and more confused with operative terminology until the transition was complete. When the Roman Empire of the West was destroyed, political power came more and more into the hands of the Church, which grew very suspicious of secret societies, and suppressed them with great vigour. She did not, however, persecute the operative Masons, whom she regarded as a body of men wisely guarding the secrets of their trade, which she supposed to be concerned with the measurements of columns and arches, quantities for the mixing of mortar, and other such things.

The Masters of the White Lodge, therefore, intentionally confused the symbolical with the operative working and thus preserved Blue Masonry, but permitted the higher wisdom to sink for the time out of sight. Thus they provided for such of the egos born in Europe as could not develop under the cruder teaching which was mis-called Christianity.

This effort to preserve the Mysteries in the Dark Ages was successful because the speculative Masons adopted as much as they could of the operative Masons' terminology, and entrusted them with some of the secrets. The latter then faithfully carried on the forms without comprehending more than half of what they meant.

Then those who held philosophical ideas of which the Church would not approve allied themselves with the operative masons, became members of the fraternity, and attended their meetings; they did not come into the guilds as operative masons, and therefore were not bound as apprentices, but were free masons accepted into the operative body, but not belonging to it by right of physical-plane work. The tradition of the Collegia passed into the Lodges of the guilds, as we shall see in the next chapter, and the ancient succession of I.M.s, which we in Britain trace through S. Alban, was handed down unbroken from century to century. In consequence of this persecution, and the partial restoration of Masonry in different forms in different countries, its outward history had been obscured and confused in the greatest possible degree. It is a matter that might no doubt be elucidated by long and painstaking research, but it would be a task involving far too great an expenditure of energy and time.

THE SYSTEM OF MITHRA

By J. S. M. Ward

While there is some doubt as to the exact number of degrees worked by the "soldiers of Mithra," it seems certain it was either seven or twelve. My own belief is that it was seven, corresponding to the seven divisions of man, the seven stars revolving round the pole star, the seven ages of the world, the seven attributes of the Deity, or the six gods and the Supreme Being.

If the seven-degree system be considered the correct form, the degrees were certainly as follows:

(1) The Lion.
(2) The Soldier (Man).
(3) The Ox.
(4) The Eagle.
(5) The Old Man, or Persian.
(6) The Gryphon.
(7) The Sun.

If we compare the names of the first four degrees with the four beasts representing the four evangelists, we shall perceive that they correspond exactly. Nor will Companion of the *Royal Arch* fail to recognise these same symbols.

Every name had a symbolic meaning, and Tertullian (*Against Marcion*, i. 18) says that "the Lions of Mithra are mysteries of an arid and scorched nature."

With the exception of the seventh degree, which corresponded with our R.A., we have little detailed knowledge of the system. We know, however, that each degree had its grips and words, its special and appropriate ceremonies, its legends, trials and final triumph of the candidate.

There was a legend of the death and burial of the Saviour and Mediator of Mankind, the Sun God Mithra, who was buried in a rock tomb and raised to life eternal. We know also that the candidate was threatened with death, and that a man (probably the candidate) appeared to be slain. This was, however, only a feigned death, and the victim, after burial in the rock tomb, was *raised* to life by the lion grip.

It would appear as if, in addition to the representation to or by every candidate of the death of Mithra, that at least once a year, at the Vernal Solstice, there was an imposing ceremony depicting the death of Mithra, which is thus described by Firmicus in *De Errore*, xxiii: "They lay a stone image by night on a bier and liturgically mourn over it, this image representing the dead god."

This symbolical corpse is in the tomb (in a cave), and after a time is withdrawn from its tomb, whereupon the worshippers rejoice ; lights are brought in and the priest anoints the *throats* of the worshippers with the words, "Be of good cheer. Ye have been instructed in the mysteries, and shall have salvation from your sorrows."

In short, this ceremony synchronised with the Christian festival of Easter. Do not let it be thought that the followers of Mithra copied the ceremony from the Christians, for there is abundant evidence that this was not so. Even the warmest contemporary partisans of Christianity, such as Tertullian, made no such claim. They admitted that the systems of Mithra were earlier than the birth of Christ, but claimed that they were a mockery inaugurated by the devil to discredit Christ's teaching.

Mithra is rock-born, (God out of the rock), and also born in a cave. In a later version He is stated to have been born of a virgin (Elisaeus, the Armenian historian, d. 480, cited by Windischmann, s. 61, 62).

It is interesting to note that the following gods are also stated to have been born in caves — Apollo, Demeter, Hercules, Hermes, and Poseidon (cf. Pausanias, iii, 25, etc.). Zeus and Dionysos were both worshipped in caves.

In each degree severe trials were imposed and real austerities demanded of the candidate. Binding oaths were exacted and penalties attached to the obligations.

In each degree there were tests and trials by water, by fire, by cold, by hunger, by thirst, by scourging, branding and by the mock menace of death.

In the second degree we know the candidate received a sword and was proclaimed a soldier of Mithra, and Tertullian tells us with unwilling admiration that the candidate in the second degree was then offered a crown, which he refused, saying "Mithra is my crown" (*De Corona*, c. xv). The candidate went through the various degrees "in order that he should become holy and passionless," and the doctrines taught included that of the expiation of and purification from sin by the aid of Mithra, "Captain of the hosts of Heaven and Saviour of Mankind"; and further, that it was because Mithra had undergone a symbolic sacrifice to secure eternal life for His worshippers that those initiated hoped also for eternal life.

Justin Martyr, in his first *Apologia*, tells us "that bread and a cup of water are placed with certain incantations in the mystic rites of one being initiated 'into the system of Mithra.' " Tertullian confirms this, and adds further information: "He also baptises his worshippers in water and makes them believe that this purifies them of their sins. . . . There Mithra sets his mark on the forehead of his soldiers, he celebrates the oblation of bread, he offers an image of the Resurrection, and presents at once the crown and the sword" (*Præscr.*, c. xl, and *De Bapt.*, c. v); and though the gospel story tells us that Jesus was born in a stable, both Origen and Justin Martyr state that He was born in a cave, and in most modem representations the scene is a cave used as a stable.

It was probably because of this fact that the ceremonies of the Order were always conducted in caves, and when natural ones could not be found, an artificial one was cut or even built. How widespread was the Order may be judged from the fact that even in that distant part of the Roman Empire known as Britain there are more remains of Mithraic temples than of Roman Christian churches.

The religion of Mithra appealed especially to the army. It is said that, like masonry, no women were admitted to its rites, but among historians there is some uncertainty as to whether there were not side degrees, at any rate, which were open to them. In any case it is certain it was pre-eminently a cult which appealed to men of the best type rather than to women.

Mithraism was a development of the old Persian faith, and we know that Artaxerxes Memnon swore "by the light of Mithra." Mithra was the Sun God, and in the Hindu Vedas He is spoken of as co-equal with Varuna and invoked as Mitra-Varuna, and in Persia Mitra-Ahura were simply the duad, or creative pair. Gradually, however, Ahura-Mazda became regarded as the Supreme Being (as is written in the Zend-Avesta), and Mithra becomes His vice-regent and captain of the hosts of Heaven in the eternal war against the destroyer Ahriman, who, unlike Shiva in India, became the embodiment of evil.

Mithra gradually developed into the mediator between God and man, and it is in this character that He becomes the most important figure in the latter Mithraic cult. The cult had embodied into it much astrological law, even the statue of the slaying of a bull, so familiar to all visitors to the British Museum, and the less well-known figure of Mithra as a lamb or ram with a cross or sword, probably have a reference to the Zodiacal signs of Taurus and Aries — though they also had other meanings — just as Piscis the fish played its part in early Christian symbolism. These three signs each refer back to the astronomical period of the point of the Equinox, which slowly shifts one house in the Zodiac every twenty-one centuries. As, for example, Christ was born at the time when the Sun at the Vernal Equinox was entering Pisces ; at the present moment it is entering Aquarius.

These and other recondite matters lie somewhat outside our subject, and must be omitted, save that we may note that the Taurobolium, or baptism in the blood of a bull, which later became associated with Mithraism, was never really part thereof, but borrowed from the Phrygians.

We fortunately know I little more about the seventh degree than we do of the first six. This was because the degree of the sun was obtained by self-initiation. The candidate had to advance himself to this degree by a ritual of meditation, fragments of which were written down; and what claimed to be the system was shown to the writer some fourteen years ago at Cambridge by a don of King's College. He has recently borrowed a copy of this work, and it proves to be a small book edited by G. R. S. Mead, and published by the Theosophical Society in 1907.

The book states that the ritual was "dug out of the chaos of the great Paris Magical Papyrus 57" (Supplement grec de la Bibliotheque Nationale), and adds that the original text has been "worked over by a school of Egyptian magicians, who inserted most of the now unintelligible words and names [*nomina arcana*], i.e. words of power. These obviously later insertions have been removed, but it must be remembered that such words were used to produce a state of hypnotic trance by their constant repetition."

Those interested in the subject should get the book, which is quite inexpensive, but the following quotation from it will prove of interest:

" . . . and thou shalt see the doors thrown open and the cosmos of the Gods that is within the doors; so that for joy and rapture of the sight thy Spirit runs to meet it and soars up. Therefore, hold thyself steady, and, gazing steadily into thyself, draw breath from the Divine. When, then, thy Soul shall be restored, say: 'Draw nigh, O Lord!' Upon this utterance His rays shall be turned on thee, and thou shalt be in the midst of them."

The ritual ends with this fine prayer, called "The Tenth Utterance":

"Hail, Lord, Thou Master of the Water! Hail, Founder of the Earth! Hail, Prince of Breath! O Lord, being born again, I pass away in being made great, and having been made great, I die.

"Being born from out the state of birth and death that giveth birth to (mortal) lives, I now, set free, pass to the state transcending birth, as Thou hast stablished it, according as Thou hast ordained and made the Mystery."

Briefly, the degree of the sun was a system which aimed at producing the Beatific Vision of the Absolute. — that state of ecstasy whereby the adept raises himself above all earthly bounds and becomes united for a moment of time with the Supreme Being. This experience, which has been described by Dante in his "Rose of the Blessed," is a spiritual experience which no human tongue can really describe. But once this state has been achieved, even if the adept returns to ordinary everyday life, all things seem changed. Earth no longer has power over him. He knows how small are human griefs and joys, how transitory all that he sees. A supreme calm has taken possession of his soul, and he is at peace. He has comprehended all that there is, was, and shall be, for he has become one with the Source of All.

In modern Europe the only place where this vision is still sought by a long course of meditation is among the monks of Mount Athos, near Salonika, hence the name by which it is usually known in the West — the Beatific Vision of Mount Athos. Even there few achieve it, but it is interesting to note that part of the *modus operandi* is to fix the eyes on the centre, or *solar plexus* and repeat over and over again certain invocations to the Deity. This supreme truth may be epitomised as follows: God is everything, and everything exists only because it is part of God. From Him all things come, and to Him all things return; Man, by a life of austerities, prayers and meditations, can raise himself out of his mortal envelope through the seven heavens, and finally become one with God. When this has been accomplished peace, founded on knowledge and comprehension, is achieved, and the soul's journey is ended. It has recovered the lost secret, and has found them at the C. of the C. This doctrine was taught by the ancient Cabbalists among the Jews, by the ancient Egyptians, by the followers of Mithra. It is still taught in all its pristine grandeur to the highest initiates among the Brahmins, and is the sublime doctrine of the Buddhists. It is the secret of the Builders of the Kaaba among the Mohammedan Dervishes. St. Paul hints at it in his epistles when he tells us he was *exalted* into the third heaven, and saw things not lawful to be uttered; and it is still remembered in the H.R. A. of Freemasonry.

Thus, having passed through the valley of the shadow, we journey on, still seeking through the vaults of the underworld, till at last our purified spirit becomes one with the Supreme Being. There at last we are able to comprehend fully His nature and our oneness with Him, which while in our finite bodies we can only dimly realise, no matter how plainly we endeavour to conceive it in our ceremony of the R.A.

THE RITES OF MITHRAS

By Manly P. Hall

When the Persian Mysteries immigrated into Southern Europe, they were quickly assimilated by the Latin mind. The cult grew rapidly, especially among the Roman soldiery, and during the Roman wars of conquest the teachings were carried by the legionaries to nearly all parts of Europe. So powerful did the cult of Mithras become that at least one Roman Emperor was initiated into the order, which met in caverns under the city of Rome. Concerning the spread of this Mystery school through different parts of Europe, C. W. King, in his Gnostics and Their Remains, says:

> "Mithraic bas-reliefs cut on the faces of rocks or on stone tablets still abound in the countries formerly the western provinces of the Roman Empire; many exist in Germany, still more in France, and in this island (Britain) they have often been discovered on the line of the Picts' Wall and the noted one at Bath."

Alexander Wilder, in his Philosophy and Ethics of the Zoroasters, states that Mithras is the Zend title for the sun, and he is supposed to dwell within that shining orb. Mithras has a male and a female aspect, though not himself androgynous. As Mithras, he is the ford of the sun, powerful and radiant, and most magnificent of the Yazatas (Izads, or Genii, of the sun). As Mithra, this deity represents the feminine principle; the mundane universe is recognized as her symbol. She represents

Nature as receptive and terrestrial, and as fruitful only when bathed in the glory of the solar orb. The Mithraic cult is a simplification of the more elaborate teachings of Zarathustra (Zoroaster), the Persian fire magician.

According to the Persians, there coexisted in eternity two principles. The first of these, Ahura-Mazda, or Ormuzd, was the Spirit of Good. From Ormuzd came forth a number of hierarchies of good and beautiful spirits (angels and archangels). The second of these eternally existing principles was called Ahriman. He was also a pure and beautiful spirit, but he later rebelled against Ormuzd, being jealous of his power. This did not occur, however, until after Ormuzd had created light, for previously Ahriman had not been conscious of the existence of Ormuzd. Because of his jealousy and rebellion, Ahriman became the Spirit of Evil. From himself he individualized a host of destructive creatures to injure Ormuzd.

When Ormuzd created the earth, Ahriman entered into its grosser elements. Whenever Ormuzd did a good deed, Ahriman placed the principle of evil within it. At last when Ormuzd created the human race, Ahriman became incarnate in the lower nature of man so that in each personality the Spirit of Good and the Spirit of Evil struggle for control. For 3,000 years Ormuzd ruled the celestial worlds with light and goodness. Then he created man. For another 3,000 years he ruled man with wisdom, and integrity. Then the power of Ahriman began, and the struggle for the soul of man continues through the next period of 3,000 years. During the fourth period of 3,000 years, the power of Ahriman will be destroyed. Good will return to the world again, evil and death will be vanquished, and at last the Spirit of Evil will bow humbly before the throne of Ormuzd. While Ormuzd and Ahriman are struggling for control of the human soul and for supremacy in Nature, Mithras, God of Intelligence, stands as mediator between the two. Many authors have noted the similarity between mercury and Mithras. As the chemical mercury acts as a solvent (according to alchemists), so Mithras seeks to harmonize the two celestial opposites.

There are many points of resemblance between Christianity and the cult of Mithras. One of the reasons for this probably is that the Persian mystics invaded Italy during the first century after Christ and the early history of both cults was closely interwoven. The Encyclopedia Britannica makes the following statement concerning the Mithraic and Christian Mysteries:

> "The fraternal and democratic spirit of the first communities, and their humble origin; the identification of the object of adoration with light and the sun; the legends of the shepherds with their gifts and adoration, the flood, and the ark; the representation in art of the fiery chariot, the drawing of water from the rock; the use of bell and candle, holy water and the communion; the sanctification of Sunday and of the 25th of December; the insistence on moral conduct, the emphasis placed on abstinence and self-control; the doctrine of heaven and hell, of primitive revelation, of the mediation of the Logos emanating from the divine, the atoning sacrifice, the constant warfare between good and evil and the final triumph of the former, the immortality of the soul, the

last judgment, the resurrection of the flesh and the fiery destruction of the universe-- [these] are some of the resemblances which, whether real or only apparent, enabled Mithraism to prolong its resistance to Christianity,"

The rites of Mithras were performed in caves. Porphyry, in his Cave of the Nymphs, states that Zarathustra (Zoroaster) was the first to consecrate a cave to the worship of God, because a cavern was symbolic of the earth, or the lower world of darkness. John P. Lundy, in his Monumental Christianity, describes the cave of Mithras as follows:

"But this cave was adorned with the signs of the zodiac, Cancer and Capricorn. The summer and winter solstices were chiefly conspicuous, as the gates of souls descending into this life, or passing out of it in their ascent to the Gods; Cancer being the gate of descent, and Capricorn of ascent. These are the two avenues of the immortals passing up and down from earth to heaven, and from heaven to earth."

The so-called chair of St. Peter, in Rome, was believed to have been used in one of the pagan Mysteries, possibly that of Mithras, in whose subterranean grottoes the votaries of the Christian Mysteries met in the early days of their faith. In Anacalypsis, Godfrey Higgins writes that in 1662, while cleaning this sacred chair of Bar-Jonas, the Twelve Labors of Hercules were discovered upon it, and that later the French discovered upon the same chair the Mohammedan confession of faith, written in Arabic.

Initiation into the rites of Mithras, like initiation into many other ancient schools of philosophy, apparently consisted of three important degrees. Preparation for these degrees consisted of self- purification, the building up of the intellectual powers, and the control of the animal nature. In the first degree the candidate was given a crown upon the point of a sword and instructed in the mysteries of Mithras' hidden power. Probably he was taught that the golden crown represented his own spiritual nature, which must be objectified and unfolded before he could truly glorify Mithras; for Mithras was his own soul, standing as mediator between Ormuzd, his spirit, and Ahriman, his animal nature. In the second degree he was given the armor of intelligence and purity and sent into the darkness of subterranean pits to fight the beasts of lust, passion, and degeneracy. In the third degree he was given a cape, upon which were drawn or woven the signs of the zodiac and other astronomical symbols. After his initiations were over, he was hailed as one who had risen from the dead, was instructed in the secret teachings of the Persian mystics, and became a full-fledged member of the order. Candidates who successfully passed the Mithraic initiations were called Lions and were marked upon their foreheads with the Egyptian cross. Mithras himself is often pictured with the head of a lion and two pairs of wings. Throughout the entire ritual were repeated references to the birth of Mithras as the Sun God, his sacrifice for man, his death that men might have eternal life, and lastly, his resurrection and the saving of all humanity by his intercession before the throne of Ormuzd. (See Heckethorn.)

While the cult of Mithras did not reach the philosophic

heights attained by Zarathustra, its effect upon the civilization of the Western world was far-reaching, for at one time nearly all Europe was converted to its doctrines. Rome, in her intercourse with other nations, inoculated them with her religious principles; and many later institutions have exhibited Mithraic culture. The reference to the "Lion" and the "Grip of the Lion's Paw" in the Master Mason's degree have a strong Mithraic tinge and may easily have originated from this cult. A ladder of seven rungs appears in the Mithraic initiation. Faber is of the opinion that this ladder was originally a pyramid of seven steps. It is possible that the Masonic ladder with seven rungs had its origin in this Mithraic symbol. Women were never permitted to enter the Mithraic Order, but children of the male sex were initiates long before they reached maturity. The refusal to permit women to join the Masonic Order may be based on the esoteric reason given in the secret instructions of the Mithraics. This cult is another excellent example of those secret societies whose legends are largely symbolic representations of the sun and his journey through the houses of the heavens. Mithras, rising from a stone, is merely the sun rising over the horizon, or, as the ancients supposed, out of the horizon, at the vernal equinox.

John O'Neill disputes the theory that Mithras was intended as a solar deity. In The Night of the Gods he writes: "The Avestan Mithra, the yazata of light, has '10,000 eyes, high, with full knowledge, strong, sleepless and ever awake.' The supreme god Ahura Mazda also has one Eye, or else it is said that 'with his eyes, the sun, moon and stars, he sees everything.' The theory that Mithra was originally a title of the supreme heavens-god--putting the sun out of court--is the only one that answers all requirements. It will be evident that here we have origins in abundance for the Freemason's Eye and 'its nunquam dormio.' " The reader must nor confuse the Persian Mithra with the Vedic Mitra. According to Alexander Wilder, "The Mithraic rites superseded the Mysteries of Bacchus, and became the foundation of the Gnostic system, which for many centuries prevailed in Asia, Egypt, and even the remote West."